Nothing stands in your way like your own hesitation - break free.

SAM PENNY
The Topify Method

topifymethod.com

Chips Investments Pty Ltd
Parcel Collect 10042 76215
Shop 4, 44 Landsborough Parade
Golden Beach QLD 4551 Australia

Chips Investments AUST

Chips Investments Pty Ltd is the publisher of this book. More information can be found at www.topifymethod.com.

Copyright © Sam Penny 2025

All rights reserved. No part of this book may be reproduced, stored in a retrieval system, or transmitted in any form or by any means—electronic, mechanical, photocopying, recording, or otherwise—without prior written permission from the publisher, except for brief quotations used in a review or critical analysis.

A CIP catalogue record for this book is available from the National Library of Australia.
ISBN 978-1-7638968-0-2

Design by Sam Penny

Chips Investments Pty Ltd is committed to sustainability. This book is printed on paper sourced from responsibly managed forests.

DEDICATION

For those looking for their next mountain to climb.

How to Use The Topify Method

Welcome to The Topify Method, your simple and effective tool for staying focused and making progress every day. This journal is designed for everyone—mums, business owners, travellers, artists—anyone looking to make the most of their time and achieve more.

At the heart of this planner is The Topify Method—a simple yet powerful system to help you align your daily actions with your bigger goals. Each Quarter, Month, Week, and Day, you'll write down your Top 5 priorities and focus on completing at least the Top 1. Small steps, taken consistently, lead to big results.

Celebrate each achievement!

SCAN TO LEARN MORE

How to Achieve More

Quarterly Focus
Write down your Top 3 Priorities for the next three months. These will guide your monthly and weekly plans to ensure every step moves you forward.

Monthly Focus
From your quarterly goals, choose the Top 5 things to accomplish this month. Keep it clear and actionable.

Weekly Focus
Break your monthly goals into smaller actions. Write down the Top 5 tasks for the week and focus on making progress.

Daily Focus
Each day, list your Top 5 tasks and commit to completing at least the Top 1. Progress comes from action.

Reflection & Looking Ahead
Take a moment at the end of each period—whether it's a day, week, month, or quarter—to reflect on your progress. What worked well? What challenges did you overcome? Celebrate your achievements, no matter how small. Then, look ahead—what's the next step to keep moving forward?

This planner is here to simplify your productivity, keep you focused, and help you achieve more—one step at a time. Let's make every day count!

SCAN TO LEARN MORE

Quarter: _____ to _____

My 3 Big Priorities This Quarter

Priority 1:

Priority 2:

Priority 3:

Why these 3?

Priority 1:

Priority 2:

Priority 3:

What Does Success Look Like?

Priority 1: _____

_____

Priority 2: _____

_____

Priority 3: _____

_____

My Top 5 for Alignment

Main Focus: _____

Consistent Action: _____

Quick Wins: _____

_____

Biggest Challenge: _____

One Rule to Follow: _____

Quarterly Commitment Statement

I commit to _____ over the next 90 days because _____

_____

Month: _____

My Top 5 for this Month

Top 1 Done

○ ☐ _____

○ ☐ _____

○ ☐ _____

○ ☐ _____

○ ☐ _____

Are these aligned with my Quarterly Top 5?

Energy flows, where focus goes.

Week Starting: _____

My Top 5 for this Week

Top 1 Done

○ ☐ _____

○ ☐ _____

○ ☐ _____

○ ☐ _____

○ ☐ _____

Are these aligned with my Monthly Top 5?

Your future self is watching - go!

My top 5 for today

Top 1 Done

○ ☐ _____

○ ☐ _____

○ ☐ _____

○ ☐ _____

○ ☐ _____

Are these aligned with my Weekly Top 5?

Perfection stands in place; progress leaps over barriers.

Date: _____   Day: _____   (1)

My top win today was: _____

Today I am grateful for: _____

My top 5 for today

Top 1 Done

○ ☐ _____

○ ☐ _____

○ ☐ _____

○ ☐ _____

○ ☐ _____

Are these aligned with my Weekly Top 5?

Lighten your mental load by jotting down your to-dos.

Date: _____ Day: _____ (2)

My top win today was: _____

Today I am grateful for: _____

My top 5 for today

Top 1   Done

○ ☐ _____

○ ☐ _____

○ ☐ _____

○ ☐ _____

○ ☐ _____

Are these aligned with my Weekly Top 5?

Perfection kills creativity; progress keeps it alive.

Date: _____ Day: _____ (3)

My top win today was: _____

Today I am grateful for: _____

My top 5 for today

Top 1 Done

○ ☐ _____

○ ☐ _____

○ ☐ _____

○ ☐ _____

○ ☐ _____

Are these aligned with my Weekly Top 5?

Perfection locks the door; progress turns the key and walks through.

Date: _____ Day: _____ (4)

My top win today was: _____

Today I am grateful for: _____

My top 5 for today

Top 1 Done

○ ☐ _____

○ ☐ _____

○ ☐ _____

○ ☐ _____

○ ☐ _____

Are these aligned with my Weekly Top 5?

Live attentively, and life rewards you
with direction and purpose.

Date: _____ Day: _____ ⑤

My top win today was: _____

Today I am grateful for: _____

My top 5 for today

Top 1 Done

○ ☐ _____

○ ☐ _____

○ ☐ _____

○ ☐ _____

○ ☐ _____

Are these aligned with my Weekly Top 5?

Live each second as if it's the secret ingredient to your dream recipe.

Date: _____   Day: _____   (6)

My top win today was: _____

Today I am grateful for: _____

My top 5 for today

Top 1 Done

○ ☐

○ ☐

○ ☐

○ ☐

○ ☐

Are these aligned with my Weekly Top 5?

Perfection never crosses the finish line—
progress does.

Date: _____ Day: _____ (7)

My top win today was: _____

Today I am grateful for: _____

Week Ending: _____

My Week in Review

My top win this week was:

_____
_____
_____

I am grateful for:

_____
_____
_____

What could be improved or learned:

_____
_____
_____

Week Starting: _____

My Top 5 for this Week

Top 1 Done

○ ☐ ....

○ ☐ ....

○ ☐ ....

○ ☐ ....

○ ☐ ....

Are these aligned with my Monthly Top 5?

Done is better than perfect.

My top 5 for today

Top 1 Done

○ ☐ _____

○ ☐ _____

○ ☐ _____

○ ☐ _____

○ ☐ _____

Are these aligned with my Weekly Top 5?

Live with purpose, and each moment becomes
a stepping stone, not a stumbling block.

Date: _____   Day: _____   (8)

My top win today was: _____

Today I am grateful for: _____

My top 5 for today

Top 1 Done
○ ☐ _____

○ ☐ _____

○ ☐ _____

○ ☐ _____

○ ☐ _____

Are these aligned with my Weekly Top 5?

In life's race, progress keeps pace;
perfection never leaves the start line.

Date: _____   Day: _____   (9)

My top win today was: _____

Today I am grateful for: _____

My top 5 for today

Top 1 Done

○ ☐ _____

○ ☐ _____

○ ☐ _____

○ ☐ _____

○ ☐ _____

Are these aligned with my Weekly Top 5?

Perfection only shines in theory;
progress glows in reality.

Date: _____ Day: _____   (10)

My top win today was: _____

Today I am grateful for: _____

My top 5 for today

Top 1 Done

○ ☐ _____

○ ☐ _____

○ ☐ _____

○ ☐ _____

○ ☐ _____

Are these aligned with my Weekly Top 5?

Look within for validation; it's the only source that's truly limitless.

Date: _____ Day: _____ (11)

My top win today was: _____

Today I am grateful for: _____

My top 5 for today

Top 1 Done

○ ☐ _____

○ ☐ _____

○ ☐ _____

○ ☐ _____

○ ☐ _____

Are these aligned with my Weekly Top 5?

Make your life lighter by letting go of what's unimportant.

Date: _____ Day: _____ (12)

My top win today was: _____

Today I am grateful for: _____

My top 5 for today

Top 1 Done

○ ☐ _____

○ ☐ _____

○ ☐ _____

○ ☐ _____

○ ☐ _____

Are these aligned with my Weekly Top 5?

Perfection robs you of daring; progress dares you to try.

Date: _____ Day: _____ (13)

My top win today was: _____

Today I am grateful for: _____

My top 5 for today

Top 1 Done

○ ☐ _____

○ ☐ _____

○ ☐ _____

○ ☐ _____

○ ☐ _____

Are these aligned with my Weekly Top 5?

Make your moment matter before it's just a memory.

Date: _____ Day: _____ (14)

My top win today was:

Today I am grateful for:

Week Ending: _____

My Week in Review

My top win this week was:

I am grateful for:

What could be improved or learned:

Week Starting: _____

My Top 5 for this Week

Top 1 Done

○ ☐ _____

○ ☐ _____

○ ☐ _____

○ ☐ _____

○ ☐ _____

Are these aligned with my Monthly Top 5?

Small steps, big results.

My top 5 for today

Top 1 Done

○ ☐ _____

○ ☐ _____

○ ☐ _____

○ ☐ _____

○ ☐ _____

Are these aligned with my Weekly Top 5?

Perfection says 'not enough'; progress says 'keep going.'

Date: _____ Day: _____ (15)

My top win today was:

Today I am grateful for:

My top 5 for today

Top 1 Done

○ □ _____

○ □ _____

○ □ _____

○ □ _____

○ □ _____

Are these aligned with my Weekly Top 5?

Stay true to your goal and flexible in your approach.

Date: _____ Day: _____ (16)

My top win today was: _____

Today I am grateful for: _____

My top 5 for today

Top 1 Done

○ ☐ _____

○ ☐ _____

○ ☐ _____

○ ☐ _____

○ ☐ _____

Are these aligned with my Weekly Top 5?

Making the most of this minute lays the foundation for every one to come.

Date: Day: (17)

My top win today was:

Today I am grateful for:

My top 5 for today

Top 1   Done

○ ☐ _____

○ ☐ _____

○ ☐ _____

○ ☐ _____

○ ☐ _____

Are these aligned with my Weekly Top 5?

Light up every space you enter with your authenticity.

Date: _____ Day: _____ (18)

My top win today was: _____

Today I am grateful for: _____

My top 5 for today

Top 1 Done

○ ☐

○ ☐

○ ☐

○ ☐

○ ☐

Are these aligned with my Weekly Top 5?

Perfection is a thief of time; progress invests it wisely.

Date: _____ Day: _____ (19)

My top win today was:

Today I am grateful for:

My top 5 for today

Top 1 Done

○ ☐ _____

○ ☐ _____

○ ☐ _____

○ ☐ _____

○ ☐ _____

Are these aligned with my Weekly Top 5?

Master your mornings to own your day.

Date: _____ Day: _____   20

My top win today was: _____

Today I am grateful for: _____

My top 5 for today

Top 1 Done

○ ☐

○ ☐

○ ☐

○ ☐

○ ☐

Are these aligned with my Weekly Top 5?

Set goals, but thrive on daily execution.

Date: _____ Day: _____ (21)

My top win today was: _____

Today I am grateful for: _____

Week Ending: _____

My Week in Review

My top win this week was:

_____
_____
_____

I am grateful for:

_____
_____
_____

What could be improved or learned:

_____
_____
_____

Week Starting: _____ (4)

My Top 5 for this Week

Top 1 Done

○ ☐ _____

○ ☐ _____

○ ☐ _____

○ ☐ _____

○ ☐ _____

Are these aligned with my Monthly Top 5?

One task. Full focus. Crush it.

My top 5 for today

Top 1 Done

○ □

○ □

○ □

○ □

○ □

Are these aligned with my Weekly Top 5?

Embrace failure as the cost of admission to success.

Date: _____   Day: _____   (22)

My top win today was: _____

Today I am grateful for: _____

My top 5 for today

Top 1   Done

○ ☐ _____

○ ☐ _____

○ ☐ _____

○ ☐ _____

○ ☐ _____

Are these aligned with my Weekly Top 5?

Let gratitude guide you, and life becomes a grand adventure.

Date: _____   Day: _____   (23)

My top win today was:

Today I am grateful for:

My top 5 for today

Top 1 Done

○ ☐ _____

○ ☐ _____

○ ☐ _____

○ ☐ _____

○ ☐ _____

Are these aligned with my Weekly Top 5?

Let go of flawless; let in forward motion.

Date: _____ Day: _____ (24)

My top win today was: _____

Today I am grateful for: _____

My top 5 for today

Top 1 Done

○ ☐ _____

○ ☐ _____

○ ☐ _____

○ ☐ _____

○ ☐ _____

Are these aligned with my Weekly Top 5?

Progress navigates obstacles; perfection is halted by them.

Date: _____ Day: _____   (25)

My top win today was: _____

Today I am grateful for: _____

My top 5 for today

Top 1   Done

○ ☐ _____

○ ☐ _____

○ ☐ _____

○ ☐ _____

○ ☐ _____

Are these aligned with my Weekly Top 5?

In the end, it's about what you do, not just what you plan.

Date: _____   Day: _____   (26)

My top win today was: _____

Today I am grateful for: _____

My top 5 for today

Top 1 Done

○ ☐ _____

○ ☐ _____

○ ☐ _____

○ ☐ _____

○ ☐ _____

Are these aligned with my Weekly Top 5?

Progress welcomes your flaws;
perfection denies your humanity.

Date: _____   Day: _____   (27)

My top win today was: _____

Today I am grateful for: _____

My top 5 for today

Top 1 Done

○ ☐ _____

○ ☐ _____

○ ☐ _____

○ ☐ _____

○ ☐ _____

Are these aligned with my Weekly Top 5?

Progress whispers 'do it anyway';
perfection shouts 'not yet.'

Date: _____   Day: _____   (28)

My top win today was: _____

Today I am grateful for: _____

Week Ending: _____

④

My Week in Review

My top win this week was:

I am grateful for:

What could be improved or learned:

Week Starting: _____

My Top 5 for this Week

Top 1 Done

○ ☐ _____

○ ☐ _____

○ ☐ _____

○ ☐ _____

○ ☐ _____

Are these aligned with my Monthly Top 5?

Win the day, every day.

My top 5 for today

Top 1 Done
○ ☐ _____

○ ☐ _____

○ ☐ _____

○ ☐ _____

○ ☐ _____

Are these aligned with my Weekly Top 5?

In the end, you're accountable for your life, not their opinions.

Date: _____ Day: _____ (29)

My top win today was: _____

Today I am grateful for: _____

My top 5 for today

Top 1 Done

○ ☐ _____

○ ☐ _____

○ ☐ _____

○ ☐ _____

○ ☐ _____

Are these aligned with my Weekly Top 5?

In the garden of life, gratitude is the flower that never withers.

Date: _____   Day: _____   (30)

My top win today was: _____

Today I am grateful for: _____

My top 5 for today

Top 1 Done

○ ☐ _____

○ ☐ _____

○ ☐ _____

○ ☐ _____

○ ☐ _____

Are these aligned with my Weekly Top 5?

Every awkward first attempt is closer to success than perfect hesitation.

Date: _____ Day: _____ (31)

My top win today was: _____

Today I am grateful for: _____

Month: _____

My Month in Review

My top win last month was:
_____
_____
_____

I am grateful for:
_____
_____
_____

What could be improved or learned:
_____
_____

Month: _____

My Top 5 for this Month

Top 1 Done
○ ☐ _____

○ ☐ _____

○ ☐ _____

○ ☐ _____

○ ☐ _____

Are these aligned with my Quarterly Top 5?

Less thinking, more doing.

Week Ending: _____

My Week in Review

My top win this week was:

_____
_____
_____

I am grateful for:

_____
_____
_____

What could be improved or learned:

_____
_____
_____

Week Starting: _____

My Top 5 for this Week

Top 1 Done

○ ☐ _____

○ ☐ _____

○ ☐ _____

○ ☐ _____

○ ☐ _____

Are these aligned with my Monthly Top 5?

Success loves speed.

My top 5 for today

Top 1 Done

○ ☐ ....

○ ☐ ....

○ ☐ ....

○ ☐ ....

○ ☐ ....

Are these aligned with my Weekly Top 5?

Indifference can be freeing—you're no longer tied to anyone else's expectations.

Date: _____ Day: _____ (1)

My top win today was: _____

Today I am grateful for: _____

My top 5 for today

Top 1 Done

○ ☐ _____

○ ☐ _____

○ ☐ _____

○ ☐ _____

○ ☐ _____

Are these aligned with my Weekly Top 5?

Every big achievement is built on small, consistent efforts.

Date: _____   Day: _____   ②

My top win today was: _____

Today I am grateful for: _____

My top 5 for today

Top 1   Done

○ ☐ _____

○ ☐ _____

○ ☐ _____

○ ☐ _____

○ ☐ _____

Are these aligned with my Weekly Top 5?

Quality work springs from consistent dedication, not random effort.

Date: _____   Day: _____   (3)

My top win today was: _____

Today I am grateful for: _____

My top 5 for today

Top 1 Done

○ ☐ _____

○ ☐ _____

○ ☐ _____

○ ☐ _____

○ ☐ _____

Are these aligned with my Weekly Top 5?

Indifference is a filter—let it remove unnecessary weight from your life.

Date: _____ Day: _____ (4)

My top win today was: _____

Today I am grateful for: _____

My top 5 for today

Top 1   Done

◯ ☐ _____

◯ ☐ _____

◯ ☐ _____

◯ ☐ _____

◯ ☐ _____

Are these aligned with my Weekly Top 5?

Initiative beats perfection
—launch and then learn.

Date: _____ Day: _____ (5)

My top win today was: _____

Today I am grateful for: _____

My top 5 for today

Top 1 Done

○ ☐ _____

○ ☐ _____

○ ☐ _____

○ ☐ _____

○ ☐ _____

Are these aligned with my Weekly Top 5?

Progress is unstoppable once you say yes; perfection says maybe forever.

Date: _____ Day: _____ (6)

My top win today was: _____

Today I am grateful for: _____

My top 5 for today

Top 1 Done

○ ☐ _____

○ ☐ _____

○ ☐ _____

○ ☐ _____

○ ☐ _____

Are these aligned with my Weekly Top 5?

Inspiration arrives when you commit to consistent doing.

Date: _____ Day: _____ (7)

My top win today was: _____

Today I am grateful for: _____

Week Ending: _____

My Week in Review

My top win this week was:

_____
_____
_____

I am grateful for:

_____
_____
_____

What could be improved or learned:

_____
_____
_____

Week Starting: _____

My Top 5 for this Week

Top 1 Done

○ ☐ _____

○ ☐ _____

○ ☐ _____

○ ☐ _____

○ ☐ _____

Are these aligned with my Monthly Top 5?

Action beats intention - start now, refine later.

My top 5 for today

Top 1   Done

○ ☐ _____

○ ☐ _____

○ ☐ _____

○ ☐ _____

○ ☐ _____

Are these aligned with my Weekly Top 5?

Quality effort outlasts momentary motivation.

Date: _____ Day: _____ (8)

My top win today was: _____

Today I am grateful for: _____

My top 5 for today

Top 1 Done

○ ☐ _____

○ ☐ _____

○ ☐ _____

○ ☐ _____

○ ☐ _____

Are these aligned with my Weekly Top 5?

Push yourself, because nobody else is going to do it for you.

Date: _____ Day: _____ (9)

My top win today was: _____

Today I am grateful for: _____

My top 5 for today

Top 1 Done
○ ☐ _____

○ ☐ _____

○ ☐ _____

○ ☐ _____

○ ☐ _____

Are these aligned with my Weekly Top 5?

It's impossible to fail at something you never begin—so start!

Date: _____   Day: _____   (10)

My top win today was:

Today I am grateful for:

My top 5 for today

Top 1 Done

○ ☐ _____

○ ☐ _____

○ ☐ _____

○ ☐ _____

○ ☐ _____

Are these aligned with my Weekly Top 5?

Let gratitude be the lens through which you see today.

Date: _____ Day: _____ (11)

My top win today was: _____

Today I am grateful for: _____

My top 5 for today

Top 1 Done

○ ☐ ....

○ ☐ ....

○ ☐ ....

○ ☐ ....

○ ☐ ....

Are these aligned with my Weekly Top 5?

Push yourself forward or get left behind
—your choice.

Date: _____ Day: _____ (12)

My top win today was: _____

Today I am grateful for: _____

My top 5 for today

Top 1 Done

○ ☐ _____

○ ☐ _____

○ ☐ _____

○ ☐ _____

○ ☐ _____

Are these aligned with my Weekly Top 5?

It's okay to be raw and real
—perfection is neither.

Date: _____ Day: _____ (13)

My top win today was: _____

Today I am grateful for: _____

My top 5 for today

Top 1 Done

○ ☐ ....

○ ☐ ....

○ ☐ ....

○ ☐ ....

○ ☐ ....

Are these aligned with my Weekly Top 5?

Push your limits; that's where your best self hides.

Date: _____   Day: _____   (14)

My top win today was: _____

Today I am grateful for: _____

Week Ending: _____

My Week in Review

My top win this week was:

_____
_____
_____

I am grateful for:

_____
_____
_____

What could be improved or learned:

_____
_____
_____

Week Starting: _____

My Top 5 for this Week

Top 1 Done

○ ☐ _____

○ ☐ _____

○ ☐ _____

○ ☐ _____

○ ☐ _____

Are these aligned with my Monthly Top 5?

Progress > Perfection - Just Start

My top 5 for today

Top 1 Done

○ ☐ _____

○ ☐ _____

○ ☐ _____

○ ☐ _____

○ ☐ _____

Are these aligned with my Weekly Top 5?

Push harder; the reward always outweighs the strain.

Date: _____ Day: _____ (15)

My top win today was: _____

Today I am grateful for: _____

My top 5 for today

Top 1 Done

○ ☐ _____

○ ☐ _____

○ ☐ _____

○ ☐ _____

○ ☐ _____

Are these aligned with my Weekly Top 5?

Keep pace with time by moving closer to your vision daily.

Date: _____ Day: _____ (16)

My top win today was: _____

Today I am grateful for: _____

My top 5 for today

Top 1 Done

○ ☐ _____

○ ☐ _____

○ ☐ _____

○ ☐ _____

○ ☐ _____

Are these aligned with my Weekly Top 5?

Keep shining, especially when the world tries to dim your light.

Date: _____ Day: _____ (17)

My top win today was:

Today I am grateful for:

My top 5 for today

Top 1 Done

○ ☐ _____

○ ☐ _____

○ ☐ _____

○ ☐ _____

○ ☐ _____

Are these aligned with my Weekly Top 5?

Push forward because you deserve better
than waiting for uncommitted support.

Date: _____ Day: _____ (18)

My top win today was: _____

Today I am grateful for: _____

My top 5 for today

Top 1   Done

○ ☐ _____

○ ☐ _____

○ ☐ _____

○ ☐ _____

○ ☐ _____

Are these aligned with my Weekly Top 5?

Keep your mind free; store your tasks where you can see them.

Date: _____ Day: _____ (19)

My top win today was: _____

Today I am grateful for: _____

My top 5 for today

Top 1 Done

○ ☐ _____

○ ☐ _____

○ ☐ _____

○ ☐ _____

○ ☐ _____

Are these aligned with my Weekly Top 5?

Pursue progress, not a pedestal of perfection.

Date: _____   Day: _____   (20)

My top win today was: _____

Today I am grateful for: _____

My top 5 for today

Top 1 Done

○ ☐ _____

○ ☐ _____

○ ☐ _____

○ ☐ _____

○ ☐ _____

Are these aligned with my Weekly Top 5?

Every completed task is a deposit in success.

Date: _____ Day: _____ (21)

My top win today was:

Today I am grateful for:

Week Ending: _____

My Week in Review

My top win this week was:

_____
_____
_____

I am grateful for:

_____
_____
_____

What could be improved or learned:

_____
_____
_____

Week Starting: _____

(9)

My Top 5 for this Week

Top 1 Done
○ ☐ _____

○ ☐ _____

○ ☐ _____

○ ☐ _____

○ ☐ _____

Are these aligned with my Monthly Top 5?

Progress beats perfection.
Take one step forward this week.

My top 5 for today

Top 1   Done

○ ☐ _____

○ ☐ _____

○ ☐ _____

○ ☐ _____

○ ☐ _____

Are these aligned with my Weekly Top 5?

Keep your mind open for ideas, but store them where you can see them.

Date: _____ Day: _____ (22)

My top win today was: _____

Today I am grateful for: _____

My top 5 for today

Top 1 Done

○ ☐ _____

○ ☐ _____

○ ☐ _____

○ ☐ _____

○ ☐ _____

Are these aligned with my Weekly Top 5?

Kick the door down on complacency
—be unstoppable today.

Date: Day: (23)

My top win today was:

Today I am grateful for:

My top 5 for today

Top 1 Done

○ ☐ _____

○ ☐ _____

○ ☐ _____

○ ☐ _____

○ ☐ _____

Are these aligned with my Weekly Top 5?

Self-discipline is the quiet force behind every success story.

Date: _____ Day: _____ (24)

My top win today was: _____

Today I am grateful for: _____

My top 5 for today

Top 1 Done

○ ☐ _____

○ ☐ _____

○ ☐ _____

○ ☐ _____

○ ☐ _____

Are these aligned with my Weekly Top 5?

Leap into the day before
doubt can catch up.

Date: _____ Day: _____   (25)

My top win today was: _____

Today I am grateful for: _____

My top 5 for today

Top 1 Done

○ ☐ _____

○ ☐ _____

○ ☐ _____

○ ☐ _____

○ ☐ _____

Are these aligned with my Weekly Top 5?

Even the grandest visions begin with focused effort right now.

Date: _____   Day: _____   (26)

My top win today was:

Today I am grateful for:

My top 5 for today

Top 1 Done

○ ☐ _____

○ ☐ _____

○ ☐ _____

○ ☐ _____

○ ☐ _____

Are these aligned with my Weekly Top 5?

Refine your present action, and your future will flourish.

Date: _____ Day: _____ (27)

My top win today was: _____

Today I am grateful for: _____

My top 5 for today

Top 1 Done

○ ☐ _____

○ ☐ _____

○ ☐ _____

○ ☐ _____

○ ☐ _____

Are these aligned with my Weekly Top 5?

Learn from your missteps; they're lessons in disguise.

Date: _____ Day: _____ (28)

My top win today was: _____

Today I am grateful for: _____

Week Ending: _____

My Week in Review

My top win this week was:

_____

_____

_____

I am grateful for:

_____

_____

_____

What could be improved or learned:

_____

_____

_____

Week Starting: _____

(10)

My Top 5 for this Week

Top 1 Done

○ ☐ _____

○ ☐ _____

○ ☐ _____

○ ☐ _____

○ ☐ _____

Are these aligned with my Monthly Top 5?

Perfection is a thief. Progress is the real prize.

My top 5 for today

Top 1   Done

○ □ _____

○ □ _____

○ □ _____

○ □ _____

○ □ _____

Are these aligned with my Weekly Top 5?

Let determination be your
daily alarm clock.

Date: _____ Day: _____ (29)

My top win today was: _____

Today I am grateful for: _____

My top 5 for today

Top 1   Done

○ ☐ _____

○ ☐ _____

○ ☐ _____

○ ☐ _____

○ ☐ _____

Are these aligned with my Weekly Top 5?

Embrace the grind
—each step sharpens your edge.

Date: _____ Day: _____ (30)

My top win today was: _____

Today I am grateful for: _____

My top 5 for today

Top 1 Done

○ ☐ _____

○ ☐ _____

○ ☐ _____

○ ☐ _____

○ ☐ _____

Are these aligned with my Weekly Top 5?

It's okay to talk, but be sure to walk the walk, too.

Date: _____ Day: _____ (31)

My top win today was: _____

Today I am grateful for: _____

Month: _____

My Month in Review

My top win last month was:

_____
_____
_____

I am grateful for:

_____
_____
_____

What could be improved or learned:

_____
_____
_____

Month: _____   (3)

My Top 5 for this Month

Top 1 Done
○ ☐ _____

○ ☐ _____

○ ☐ _____

○ ☐ _____

○ ☐ _____

Are these aligned with my Quarterly Top 5?

Chasing perfection steals your time—
progress pays the real rewards.

Week Ending: _____

My Week in Review

My top win this week was:

_____
_____
_____

I am grateful for:

_____
_____
_____

What could be improved or learned:

_____
_____
_____

Week Starting: _____

My Top 5 for this Week

Top 1 Done

○ ☐ _____

○ ☐ _____

○ ☐ _____

○ ☐ _____

○ ☐ _____

Are these aligned with my Monthly Top 5?

Perfection steals momentum. Progress builds success.

My top 5 for today

Top 1   Done

○ ☐ _____

○ ☐ _____

○ ☐ _____

○ ☐ _____

○ ☐ _____

Are these aligned with my Weekly Top 5?

Progress checks things off; perfection checks you out.

Date: _____   Day: _____   ①

My top win today was: _____

Today I am grateful for: _____

My top 5 for today

Top 1 Done

○ ☐ _____

○ ☐ _____

○ ☐ _____

○ ☐ _____

○ ☐ _____

Are these aligned with my Weekly Top 5?

Progress embraces each stumble;
perfection fears every flaw.

Date: _____   Day: _____   (2)

My top win today was: _____

Today I am grateful for: _____

My top 5 for today

Top 1 Done

○ ☐ _____

○ ☐ _____

○ ☐ _____

○ ☐ _____

○ ☐ _____

Are these aligned with my Weekly Top 5?

Productive minds turn obstacles into opportunities.

Date: _____ Day: _____ ③

My top win today was: _____

Today I am grateful for: _____

My top 5 for today

Top 1 Done

○ ☐ _____

○ ☐ _____

○ ☐ _____

○ ☐ _____

○ ☐ _____

Are these aligned with my Weekly Top 5?

Mindfulness today stabilizes a direction for tomorrow.

Date: _____   Day: _____   (4)

My top win today was: _____

Today I am grateful for: _____

My top 5 for today

Top 1   Done

◯ ☐ _____

◯ ☐ _____

◯ ☐ _____

◯ ☐ _____

◯ ☐ _____

Are these aligned with my Weekly Top 5?

Satisfaction is the fruit of sweat
—get to work.

Date: _____   Day: _____   (5)

My top win today was: _____

Today I am grateful for: _____

My top 5 for today

Top 1 Done

◯ ☐ _____

◯ ☐ _____

◯ ☐ _____

◯ ☐ _____

◯ ☐ _____

Are these aligned with my Weekly Top 5?

Moments given purpose can alter your entire trajectory.

Date: _____ Day: _____ (6)

My top win today was: _____

Today I am grateful for: _____

My top 5 for today

Top 1 Done

○ ☐ _____

○ ☐ _____

○ ☐ _____

○ ☐ _____

○ ☐ _____

Are these aligned with my Weekly Top 5?

Progress happens one focused step at a time.

Date: _____ Day: _____ (7)

My top win today was: _____

Today I am grateful for: _____

Week Ending: _____

My Week in Review

My top win this week was:

_____
_____
_____

I am grateful for:

_____
_____
_____

What could be improved or learned:

_____
_____
_____

Week Starting: _____

My Top 5 for this Week

Top 1 Done

○ ☐ _____

○ ☐ _____

○ ☐ _____

○ ☐ _____

○ ☐ _____

Are these aligned with my Monthly Top 5?

Own the week—start strong, finish stronger.

My top 5 for today

Top 1 Done

○ ☐ _____

○ ☐ _____

○ ☐ _____

○ ☐ _____

○ ☐ _____

Are these aligned with my Weekly Top 5?

Risking failure is the only way to discover success.

Date: _____ Day: _____ (8)

My top win today was: _____

Today I am grateful for: _____

My top 5 for today

Top 1 Done

○ ☐ _____

○ ☐ _____

○ ☐ _____

○ ☐ _____

○ ☐ _____

Are these aligned with my Weekly Top 5?

Own your flaws—they're part of your unique design.

Date: _____ Day: _____ (9)

My top win today was: _____

Today I am grateful for: _____

My top 5 for today

Top 1 Done

○ □ _____

○ □ _____

○ □ _____

○ □ _____

○ □ _____

Are these aligned with my Weekly Top 5?

Own your worth: only you can define how valuable you truly are.

Date: _____ Day: _____ (10)

My top win today was: _____

Today I am grateful for: _____

My top 5 for today

Top 1   Done

○ ☐ ....

○ ☐ ....

○ ☐ ....

○ ☐ ....

○ ☐ ....

Are these aligned with my Weekly Top 5?

Even small wins cast
long shadows of success.

Date: _____ Day: _____   (11)

My top win today was: _____

Today I am grateful for: _____

My top 5 for today

Top 1   Done

○ ☐ _____

○ ☐ _____

○ ☐ _____

○ ☐ _____

○ ☐ _____

Are these aligned with my Weekly Top 5?

Pare life down to essentials—only then
can real productivity thrive.

Date: _____ Day: _____ (12)

My top win today was: _____

Today I am grateful for: _____

My top 5 for today

Top 1 Done

○ ☐ _____

○ ☐ _____

○ ☐ _____

○ ☐ _____

○ ☐ _____

Are these aligned with my Weekly Top 5?

Progress is a quiet champion;
perfection is a loud thief.

Date: _____ Day: _____ (13)

My top win today was: _____

Today I am grateful for: _____

My top 5 for today

Top 1 Done

○ ☐ _____

○ ☐ _____

○ ☐ _____

○ ☐ _____

○ ☐ _____

Are these aligned with my Weekly Top 5?

Energy doesn't come to you
—generate it through action.

Date: _____ Day: _____ (14)

My top win today was:

Today I am grateful for:

Week Ending: _____

My Week in Review

My top win this week was:

_____
_____
_____

I am grateful for:

_____
_____
_____

What could be improved or learned:

_____
_____
_____

Week Starting: _____

My Top 5 for this Week

Top 1   Done
○ □ ....

○ □ ....

○ □ ....

○ □ ....

○ □ ....

Are these aligned with my Monthly Top 5?

Every day is a step forward—stack them wisely.

My top 5 for today

Top 1 Done

○ ☐ _____

○ ☐ _____

○ ☐ _____

○ ☐ _____

○ ☐ _____

Are these aligned with my Weekly Top 5?

People may walk away, but your determination will remain if you choose it.

Date: _____ Day: _____ (15)

My top win today was: _____

Today I am grateful for: _____

My top 5 for today

Top 1　Done

○ ☐ _____

○ ☐ _____

○ ☐ _____

○ ☐ _____

○ ☐ _____

Are these aligned with my Weekly Top 5?

Perfect isn't coming; act on what you can do now.

Date: _____ Day: _____ (16)

My top win today was: _____

Today I am grateful for: _____

My top 5 for today

Top 1   Done

○ ☐ _____

○ ☐ _____

○ ☐ _____

○ ☐ _____

○ ☐ _____

Are these aligned with my Weekly Top 5?

Progress is built with every small action you refuse to skip.

Date: _____ Day: _____ (17)

My top win today was: _____

Today I am grateful for: _____

My top 5 for today

Top 1 Done

○ ☐ _____

○ ☐ _____

○ ☐ _____

○ ☐ _____

○ ☐ _____

Are these aligned with my Weekly Top 5?

Perfection blinds you to the beauty of steady improvement.

Date: _____ Day: _____ (18)

My top win today was: _____

Today I am grateful for: _____

My top 5 for today

Top 1 Done

◯ ☐ _____

◯ ☐ _____

◯ ☐ _____

◯ ☐ _____

◯ ☐ _____

Are these aligned with my Weekly Top 5?

Progress is made by movers, not bystanders—start moving.

Date: _____ Day: _____   (19)

My top win today was: _____

Today I am grateful for: _____

My top 5 for today

Top 1 Done

○ ☐

○ ☐

○ ☐

○ ☐

○ ☐

Are these aligned with my Weekly Top 5?

Progress is motion; perfection is a mirage on the horizon.

Date: _____ Day: _____ (20)

My top win today was: _____

Today I am grateful for: _____

My top 5 for today

Top 1 Done

○ ☐ _____

○ ☐ _____

○ ☐ _____

○ ☐ _____

○ ☐ _____

Are these aligned with my Weekly Top 5?

Perfection is a security blanket that smothers growth.

Date: _____ Day: _____ (21)

My top win today was: _____

Today I am grateful for: _____

Week Ending: _____

My Week in Review

My top win this week was:

I am grateful for:

What could be improved or learned:

Week Starting: _____   (14)

My Top 5 for this Week

Top 1 Done
○ ☐ _____

○ ☐ _____

○ ☐ _____

○ ☐ _____

○ ☐ _____

Are these aligned with my Monthly Top 5?

Win the morning, win the week.

My top 5 for today

Top 1   Done

○ ☐ _____

○ ☐ _____

○ ☐ _____

○ ☐ _____

○ ☐ _____

Are these aligned with my Weekly Top 5?

Perfection is a thief of beginnings—start imperfectly and grow boldly.

Date: _____   Day: _____   (22)

My top win today was: _____

Today I am grateful for: _____

My top 5 for today

Top 1 Done

○ ☐ ....

○ ☐ ....

○ ☐ ....

○ ☐ ....

○ ☐ ....

Are these aligned with my Weekly Top 5?

Progress is the diamond; perfection is just the unmined rock.

Date: Day: (23)

My top win today was:

Today I am grateful for:

My top 5 for today

Top 1 Done

○ ☐ _____

○ ☐ _____

○ ☐ _____

○ ☐ _____

○ ☐ _____

Are these aligned with my Weekly Top 5?

Organize your day like an architect, then build it like a craftsman.

Date: _____   Day: _____   (24)

My top win today was:

Today I am grateful for:

My top 5 for today

Top 1 Done

○ □ _____

○ □ _____

○ □ _____

○ □ _____

○ □ _____

Are these aligned with my Weekly Top 5?

Progress is the steady path; perfection is the false horizon.

Date: _____ Day: _____   (25)

My top win today was: _____

Today I am grateful for: _____

My top 5 for today

Top 1 Done

○ ☐ _____

○ ☐ _____

○ ☐ _____

○ ☐ _____

○ ☐ _____

Are these aligned with my Weekly Top 5?

Progress is built on trying;
perfection is built on stalling.

Date: _____ Day: _____   (26)

My top win today was: _____

Today I am grateful for: _____

My top 5 for today

Top 1 Done

○ □ _____

○ □ _____

○ □ _____

○ □ _____

○ □ _____

Are these aligned with my Weekly Top 5?

Perfection robs you of momentum; keep moving, even if it's not perfect.

Date: _____ Day: _____ (27)

My top win today was: _____

Today I am grateful for: _____

My top 5 for today

Top 1   Done

○ ☐ _____

○ ☐ _____

○ ☐ _____

○ ☐ _____

○ ☐ _____

Are these aligned with my Weekly Top 5?

Persistence polishes potential into productivity.

Date: _____ Day: _____ (28)

My top win today was: _____

Today I am grateful for: _____

Week Ending: _____ (14)

My Week in Review

My top win this week was:

_____
_____
_____

I am grateful for:

_____
_____
_____

What could be improved or learned:

_____
_____
_____

Week Starting: _____

My Top 5 for this Week

Top 1 Done

○ ☐ _____

○ ☐ _____

○ ☐ _____

○ ☐ _____

○ ☐ _____

Are these aligned with my Monthly Top 5?

A productive week starts with a single focused task.

My top 5 for today

Top 1   Done

○ ☐ _____

○ ☐ _____

○ ☐ _____

○ ☐ _____

○ ☐ _____

Are these aligned with my Weekly Top 5?

Stop hitting snooze on your goals—time to show up for yourself.

Date: _____   Day: _____   (29)

My top win today was: _____

Today I am grateful for: _____

My top 5 for today

Top 1 Done
○ ☐

○ ☐

○ ☐

○ ☐

○ ☐

Are these aligned with my Weekly Top 5?

Plan carefully, but remember: plans alone don't produce results.

Date: _____ Day: _____   (30)

My top win today was:

Today I am grateful for:

My top 5 for today

Top 1   Done

○ ☐

○ ☐

○ ☐

○ ☐

○ ☐

Are these aligned with my Weekly Top 5?

Stop letting your ideas collect dust—
release them into action.

Date: _____ Day: _____ (31)

My top win today was: _____

Today I am grateful for: _____

Quarter: _____ to _____

My 3 Big Priorities This Quarter

Priority 1:

Priority 2:

Priority 3:

How Did I Go on My Big 3?

Priority 1:

Priority 2:

Priority 3:

Perfection is a thief.

SAM PENNY
The Topify Method

topifymethod.com

Notes

www.ingramcontent.com/pod-product-compliance
Lightning Source LLC
Chambersburg PA
CBHW070043230426
43661CB00005B/743